Abdullahi Hussaini

The Impact of Multinational Corporations On Nigeria's Economy:

D1783949

Abdullahi Hussaini

The Impact of Multinational Corporations On Nigeria's Economy:

A study of Peugeot Automobile Nigeria

LAP LAMBERT Academic Publishing

Impressum/Imprint (nur für Deutschland/only for Germany)
Bibliografische Information der Deutschen Nationalbibliothek: Die Deutsche Nationalbibliothek verzeichnet diese Publikation in der Deutschen Nationalbibliografie; detaillierte bibliografische Daten sind im Internet über http://dnb.d-nb.de abrufbar.
Alle in diesem Buch genannten Marken und Produktnamen unterliegen warenzeichen-, marken- oder patentrechtlichem Schutz bzw. sind Warenzeichen oder eingetragene Warenzeichen der jeweiligen Inhaber. Die Wiedergabe von Marken, Produktnamen, Gebrauchsnamen, Handelsnamen, Warenbezeichnungen u.s.w. in diesem Werk berechtigt auch ohne besondere Kennzeichnung nicht zu der Annahme, dass solche Namen im Sinne der Warenzeichen- und Markenschutzgesetzgebung als frei zu betrachten wären und daher von jedermann benutzt werden dürften.

Coverbild: www.ingimage.com

Verlag: LAP LAMBERT Academic Publishing GmbH & Co. KG
Heinrich-Böcking-Str. 6-8, 66121 Saarbrücken, Deutschland
Telefon +49 681 3720-310, Telefax +49 681 3720-3109
Email: info@lap-publishing.com

Herstellung in Deutschland:
Schaltungsdienst Lange o.H.G., Berlin
Books on Demand GmbH, Norderstedt
Reha GmbH, Saarbrücken
Amazon Distribution GmbH, Leipzig
ISBN: 978-3-8473-0930-7

Imprint (only for USA, GB)
Bibliographic information published by the Deutsche Nationalbibliothek: The Deutsche Nationalbibliothek lists this publication in the Deutsche Nationalbibliografie; detailed bibliographic data are available in the Internet at http://dnb.d-nb.de.
Any brand names and product names mentioned in this book are subject to trademark, brand or patent protection and are trademarks or registered trademarks of their respective holders. The use of brand names, product names, common names, trade names, product descriptions etc. even without a particular marking in this works is in no way to be construed to mean that such names may be regarded as unrestricted in respect of trademark and brand protection legislation and could thus be used by anyone.

Cover image: www.ingimage.com

Publisher: LAP LAMBERT Academic Publishing GmbH & Co. KG
Heinrich-Böcking-Str. 6-8, 66121 Saarbrücken, Germany
Phone +49 681 3720-310, Fax +49 681 3720-3109
Email: info@lap-publishing.com

Printed in the U.S.A.
Printed in the U.K. by (see last page)
ISBN: 978-3-8473-0930-7

DEDICATION

Dedicated to my daughter Karima Abdullahi Hussaini.

TABLE OF CONTENTS

CHAPTER FOUR

4.0 Impact of PAN

4.1 PAN and Import Substitution

4.2 PAN and Employment

CHAPTER FIVE

5.0 Summary, Conclusion and Recommendation

5.1 Summary

5.2 Conclusion

5.3 Recommendation

Bibliography

LIST OF TABLES

ACKNOWLEDGEMENT

First and forermos my thanks and gratitude goes to Allah (swt) for making it possible for me to complete this project.

I wish to acknowledge the contribution of Dr. Habu Mohammed Fagge of Bayero University.

I am grateful to Mohammed Sani Tafida who has done similar work and equally contributed to this work.

My sincere appreciation to my wife, mother , children and all my friends for their contributions.

May Allah reward him abundantly, Amin.

CHAPTER ONE

INTRODUCTION

Multinational corporations are business entities that operate in more than one country. Multinational corporations (MNCs) have been a source of controversy ever since the East India Company developed the British taste for tea and a Chinese taste for opium (John 1998). A typical multinational corporation (MNC) normally functions with a headquarters that is based in one country, while other facilities are based in locations in other countries. In some circles, a multinational corporation is referred to as a multinational enterprise (MNE) or a transnational corporation (TNC) (Tatum, 2010). The idea of multinational corporations has been around for centuries but in the second half of the twentieth century multinational corporations have become very important enterprises. Tatum proposes that multinationals operate in different structural models. The first and common model is for the multinational corporation positioning its executive headquarters in one nation, while production facilities are located in one or more other countries. This model often allows the company to take advantage of benefits of incorporating in a given locality, while also being able to produce goods and services in areas where the cost of production is lower. The second structural model is for a MNC to base the parent company in one nation and operate subsidiaries in other countries around the world. With this model, just about all the functions of the parent are based in the country of origin. The subsidiaries more or less function independently, outside of a few basic ties to the parent. A third approach to the setup of an MNC involves the establishment of a headquarters in one country that oversees a diverse conglomeration that stretches to many different countries and industries (Tatum2010; Robinson 1979). With this model, the MNC includes affiliates, subsidiaries and possibly evensome facilities that report directly to the headquarters. Such direct investment means the extension of

5

the managerial control across national boundaries (Gilpin, 1987). Rugman et al (1985), who prefer to use the name multinational enterprises, say that the concept of the MNE is that "the difference between Domestic Corporation and the MNE is that the latter operates across national boundaries". While institutions are important for economic development, particularly in resource rich countries, the interaction between multinational corporations and host country institutions is not well understood (Wiig and Kolstad, (2010). There is a risk that multinational corporations facilitate patronage problems in resource rich countries, exacerbating the resource curse. Multinational corporations (MNCs) in service industries have given this sector's large and growing impact on the global economy (Goerzen and Makino, 2007). The Marxists view the emergence of the multinational corporations as a historically progressive aspect of capitalism in the process of developing, at international level (Gilpin 1987; Stopford 1988). In all these views both Marxist and non-Marxist, the common basis is productive activity in more than one social formation. Another point to be noted right away is that in a social formation there may be many multinationals with different nationalities and also many corporations of the same nationality. In a social formation where there are many MNCs from different nations, there are higher possibilities of conflicts than where they are mainly from the same country. The nature or objective of MNCs is maximization of profit at the lowest possible cost. Actually it is this feature that gave rise to MNCs. So the idea of investing in foreign land is not to better the lot of the host nation but to exploit as much as is possible in order to develop the home country. Presently multinational corporations have dominated discussion on political economy. Activities of the MNCs in Nigeria have generated a repulsive reaction from many economic theorists like (Onimode 1982). Onimode regards MNCs as monsters that have consistently and systematically stultified economicdevelopment in various parts of the world. The merits as well as the demerits of the MNCs in Nigeria, the consequences of economic exploitation of MNCs in Nigeria and suggest ways for restitution.

Nigeria has a population of over 140 million people and abundance of natural resources, especially hydrocarbons, it is among the 10th largest oil producer in the world and the most prolific oil producer in Sub-Saharan- Africa. The Nigerian economy is largely dependent on its oil sector which supplies 95% of its foreign earnings and the downstream oil industry happens to be another key sector.

Despite the strategic significance of steel in the industrialization of a nation, Nigeria iron and steel sector remains in comatose, characterised by negligible local production and low return on investment, despite the abundance of local raw materials required for the production of primary steel such as limestone, iron ore, and coal. The absence of a functional steel industry significantly limits the growth of manufacturing sector and stalls rapid development of skill and technology required to drive industrial growth.

Like all raw material producing states, Nigeria is an area that attracts foreign investment With its economic and social status as a developing nation, the outlook of its economy is agrarian in nature. The country is rich in terms of natural resources.

Nigeria was a colonial state under British control, domination and exploitation. At a political independence in 1960, Nigeria emerged as a neo-colonial state. Although the country is no longer a colony, its economic, political, social and educational institutions are structured along western capitalist model. The Nigerian political economy is subject to imperialist control of the western world and it is integrated into the international capitalist economic system, which serve the interest of the international capitalist economies.

The dominant mode of conceiving the structure of the Nigerian economy is by visualizing it in terms of the relationship between the outputs of the various sectors of the economy such as industrial, agricultural, mining and quarrying, building and construction sectors, telecommunication, transportation, etc.

The structure of the Nigerian economy can therefore be conceived in its neo-colonial capitalist nature in which the clientele class or the national bourgeoisies and compradors exercise dominant influence on the economic life and activities of majority of Nigerians. They do such through the state, relations with the western bourgeoisie and activities of the multi-national corporations (MNCs), which dominate major sectors of the economy. The mining and quarrying sector is one of the sectors where the forces of imperialism are dominant. The domination of this sector by foreign business interests is highly pronounced. The discovery of oil as the major foreign exchange earner in the 70s attracted mining multi-national oil companies to expand the scope of their oil exploration and exploitation of petroleum resources in Nigeria. These foreign companies possess technology to engage in such operations efficiently. However, this had led to the dependence of the Nigerian economy on foreign technology and inputs belonging to the advanced capitalist states.

The manufacturing and crafts sector is also dominated by the multi-nationals. In 1966 for instance, foreign investors in manufacturing sector controlled 81.5% as against 18.5% by Nigerians (National Institute for International Affairs (NIIA), 19997). In 1970, foreign investment controlled 57.3% while Nigerians controlled 42.7%, and in 1976 also foreign domination continued even after the indigenization decree had been promulgated; the foreign investors controlled 56.7% as against 43.3% controlled by Nigerians (National Institute for International Affairs). Most of the multi-national (United African Company, Unilever groups and so on) controlling this sector relies heavily on foreign inputs for its survival. The manufacturing industries import almost all they need in order to be in production (O. Onido, NIIA, 1987). They import raw materials and machinery needed for their production. Its heavy reliance on foreign resources has led to its being described as sector consisting of mere assembly plants for foreign goods.

One of the most relevant examples of the above scenario and a case study of this research project is the automobile industry. Only three companies dominate these sectors and all are multi-nationals. This means that multi-national corporations dominate the automobile industry. This industry heavily relies on foreign inputs and technology for its operations. Among these companies- ANAMCO, Volkswagen and Peugeot Automobile Nigeria (PAN), none produces automobile; they merely assemble. PAN remains the surviving automobile company in Nigeria and its presence has adversely affected the nation's balance of payments, industrialization inter-alia which this research will examine in subsequent chapters.

Nigeria's economic dependence has been deeply entrenched through huge foreign investments, the solicitation and acceptance of foreign technical assistance and loan from external sources and maintenance of cultural, social and educational ties. The implications of Nigeria's economic dependence are far reaching and devastating. Firstly, it easily permits the numerous investors to repatriate their huge profit thereby helping to develop their own countries and in the process, under developing the host countries.

The structure of the Nigerian economy therefore, encourages imperialist domination and exploitation, which increases distributional inequalities and mass poverty through some instruments like MNCs that exploit cheap labour and extract profit through surplus value and international division of labour.

With reference to the natural resources that have been identified and being exploited, the country's benefit from the exploitation have not been maximized as a result of the method of exploitation and utilization. Most of the resources are explored and exploited by foreign companies (under certain agreements), sold cheaply and exported to foreign countries as raw materials where they are being processed into finished goods and then imported by Nigeria at an exorbitant prices. During the exploration and exploitation of the resources, Nigerians are employed as daily paid or as junior staff at relatively cheap wages. The machinery used in the exploration and exploitation are imported at high costs. Management is usually in the hands of these foreigners commonly called experts, earning very high salaries.

1.1 STATEMENT OF THE PROBLEM

Multi-national Corporations (MNCs) are believed to be the major sources of absolute repatriation of capital and agents for impeding local production capacity and technology.

MNCs are also believed to be exploiting local labour in the host country and hence the under-development of the host economy, which has entailed increasing social inequality.

With Peugeot Automobile Nigeria (PAN) the case study of this research, the following problems are outlined through the following questions:

- Has PAN introduced and improved indigenous technology within the industry in Nigeria through technology transfer?
- Has the company invested in Research and Development (R&D) that allows technological innovations?
- Has the company aided in the industrialization process of Nigeria?
- Is Nigeria economy benefitting from the revenue generated by PAN?

On dealing with these issues the emphasis is on industrialization, capital flow, and technology transfer and employment creation.

1.2 OBJECTIVES OF THE STUDY

The objectives of this study are:

- To examine the impact of Peugeot Automobile Nigeria (PAN) on the economy of Nigeria.
- To examine whether locally produced components are included in Peugeot vehicle manufacturing and at what percentage.
- To assess whether technology has been transferred and to what extent.

1.3 SIGNIFICANCE OF THE STUDY

The significance of the study is to examine the activities of PAN and to evaluate its contribution to the development of Nigeria's economy in relation to industrialization.

This study is equally significant in terms of assessing whether the Multi-National corporations (MNCs) are agents of development or agents of exploitation.

1.4 RESEARCH METHODOLOGY

This research will generate its data from primary and secondary sources. The primary source shall consist of interviews with personnel of various departments of the company.

The secondary source shall consist of content analysis from consultation with newspapers, magazines and pamphlets containing exclusive information about the company.

1.5 THEORETICAL FRAMEWORK

Nigeria was a British colony, which gained independence in 1960. During the period of colonialism, the colonial masters introduced programs and policies to the Nigerian economy. These programs inter-alia were the establishment of MNCs which will engineer trade between the host country Nigeria and the home country in Europe; and making Nigeria a primary producer of raw material for their industries.

It is against this background that this research will adopt dependency theory as it analytical tool. Dependency theory seeks to explain why former colonies are under developed through exploitation by the advanced capitalist economies. This means despite abundant raw materials in Nigeria and the establishments of the MNCs, the country is still backward.

The varieties of dependency theories combine elements of traditional Marxism with economic nationalism. Dependency theorist takes their analysis of capitalism particularly Marxist theory of capitalist imperialism and their concern with domestic distribution of wealth from Marxism. Advocates of dependency theory differ in their definition of precise mechanism that has brought about under development. The general positions regarding the relationship of the advanced capitalist to less developed economies can be placed into three categories:

- The Exploitation theory (which is our concern in this study)
- The doctrine of imperial neglect and
- The concept of dependent development

The "exploitation" theory maintains that the third world is poor because it has been systematically exploited (Amin, 1976). The under development of the third world is functionally related to the development of the core and modern world system, has permitted

12

the advanced core to drain the periphery of its economic surplus, transferring from less developed capitalist economy through the mechanism of trade investment (MNCs). In the advanced capitalist economies markets have become very competitive, the human resources within these economies have been exhausted, markets for their commodities is no longer available. So there was urgent need for firms to go internationally, establish subsidiaries in the third world economies where labour is cheap and inability to produce because of lack of technology will also need foreign commodities.

The link between this adopted theory and this research study emanates from the fact that France, the home country of Automobile Peugeot (AP) is an advanced capitalist economy. This AP Company has a subsidiary in third world economy, Nigeria which has the market and cheap labour to be exploited by France.

Exploitation is necessary for capitalist development. The parent company AP is in competition within the French economy. Investing where there are cheap labour and markets is very necessary for their products so as to appropriate more capital. Despite the assumed technologies introduced by France to Nigeria, the latter is still backward in technology, despite the capital flow the Nigerian economy gains little. In essence, France exploits Nigeria's economy through PAN.

1.6 THE SCOPE OF THE STUDY

The scope of the study will focus on Peugeot Automobile Nigeria (PAN) a multi-national company with its parent company in France. PAN is just a mere assembly plant while AP France manufactures the car components.

The study will assess the implication of foreign technology, locally sourced components and capital required for the company's operations.

13

1.7 DEFINITION OF CONCEPTS

- FOREIGN DIRECT INVESTMENT

  Foreign investment is defined as the movement of capital either productive machinery or cash from one economy to another or several economies, for the purpose of making available service and commodities where they are needed and reciprocally where the market exist. Foreign investment could be in form of port folio or foreign direct investment like the establishment of MNCs.

- MULTI-NATIONAL CORPORATION

  A multi-national corporation may be defined as an enterprise having a home base in one country, together with related facilities in the other countries. It could also be a business enterprise organized in one society with activities abroad growing out of direct investment. Typically, an MNC consists of the parent company and wholly or partially owned subsidiaries located abroad.

- CAPITAL

  Capital is any value or economic asset, which needed to generate more wealth or more accurately, surplus value. Capital is also a self-augmenting value. Capital can also be defined as productive means of production that is commodities that have been produced and which are themselves in the production of other commodities. There are fixed capital machinery and circulating capital like semi-finished products.

1.8 ORGANIZATION

The first chapter begins with the introduction which entails the structure of the Nigerian economy linked to the automobile industry. The statement of problem, objective of the study, research methodology, theoretical framework, scope of the study, the definition of terms are all contained in the first chapter.

The second chapter will basically consist of the review of relevant literatures.

The third chapter shall consist the impact of PAN on the development of Nigeria. These areas include; technology transfer, employment creation and also the political economy analysis.

The last chapter will dwell on the summary, conclusion and recommendation.

CHAPTER TWO

2.0 LITERATURE REVIEW

Over the years multi-national corporations (MNCs) have grown dramatically in size and influence in the expanding economy. Consequently MNCs have become the objects of considerable discussion and animosity (R.E Muller and R.J Barnet, 1974). G.W Ball (1971) coined the term 'Cosmocorp' to suggest those entities increasing power in the international arena; R. Gilpin (1975) has attributed United State's power to the MNCs; D.H Blake and R.S Walters (1987) ask the often posed question whether MNC is a growth or under development for host countries and A. Sampson (1975) has exposed the oligopolistic aspirations of the major oil companies known as the seven sisters. Operating atimes with resources that often exceed the GNP of its host country and in certain industries (notably oil), participating in cartels designed to control prices and production internationally, the MNC is both a source of capital investment and a threat to the nation states.

The MNCs according to Marx rose as a result of the rise of new age of capitalism, which Lenin called "Imperialism": the highest stage of capitalism. These MNCs that arose represented a more developed stage on the concentration of production and circulation of both goods and capital. The MNCs took the form of direct investment, which replaced portfolio investment. In 1914, 90% in all international capital movement took the form of portfolio investment by individuals and financial oligarchies, now 75% of capital outflows are in the form of direct investment entailing control of ventures (D. Nabudere, 1977).

Some workers have drawn parallels between the new MNCs and the earlier mercantilist international firms, which are medici of Florence, Genoa and Venice in the 13th century,

16

the Grosse ravensburgge Sellschaft in the 15th century, Germany and and fuggers in Augsburg, were family business in two or three countries under the very different conditions of feudalist Europe. The MNCs of today are really a new phase internationally business organization which can only be properly understood in the context of the development of capitalist system (D. Nabudere, 1977)

Historically, the United States has been the home country for the largest proportion of parent companies, followed by Britain and West Germany. Furthermore, although the growth of MNCs is a global phenomenon, if the magnitude of foreign direct investment is used to measure their global reach, it is apparent that the major part of all transnational business is located in the developed areas making up the first world. Practically, all foreign direct investment originate in developed market economies, which also absorb more than three quarters of all investment flows (commission on TNCs, 19860). The developing countries share of foreign direct investment grew in the 1970s, but it plummeted during the debt crisis of the 1980s (centre on TNCs, 1986).

Another development in the global pattern of foreign direct investment is the emergence of Japan as a major home country. The outflow of Japanese foreign direct investment increase nearly fourfold between 1975 and 1985, moving from $3.3 billion to $12.2 billion during that period (Centre on TNCs, 1987-9).

The growing number and economic clout of MNCs contribute to the controversy surrounding their impact. It has been estimated that in the early 1980s about eighteen thousand MNCs worldwide controlled assets in two or more countries and that these corporations were responsible for marketing roughly about four-fifths of the world's trade (excluding that of the centrally planned economies). Between 1960 and 1980 the revenues of the two top hundred multi-national firms escalated as their combined share of the world's gross domestic product (GDP) increased from 18 to 29 percent (Clair Monte and Cavanaugh, 1982: 149, 152, 155).

The main characteristic identifying the MNC is its central direction. The plan is drawn up in the headquarters and the activities of the subsidiary are tightly integrated with each other. The availability of goods, international communication, air services, telephone, teleprinter and telex services as well as computers became vital to the MNCs. Most MNCS are open about their motives. They point out that corporations goes transnational to preserve and expand markets in areas protected by trade barriers, to provide consumers with the goods produced in home country, to take advantage of economic scale and comparatively lower prices than export; to search for raw materials and cheap labour if this will contribute to general efficiency and to obtain knowledge cheaply by calling on local enterprises.

The MNC, must however, always seek to obtain profits greater than average profits, in order to obtain profits greater than average profits. In order for a country to go overseas, it must be in position to make higher profits there than it can in domestic market. This is the central motive for the MNC, which determines the criteria for its investments decisions. It is generally true to say that most MNCs make a general survey on the size of the market, investment climate, cost (production, transportation and resource factors), profitability, payback period and average rate of return before investing in particular economy. As far as the market is concerned, the corporation will try to determine the present and protective growth of demand and their share to this market. They would naturally consider whether they can attain sufficient scales for economic production and a satisfactory level of profit. To help them come to such conclusion, they will analyse a country's gross national product (GNP) and gross domestic product (GDP), population and its distribution, industrial production, production of specific sectors of the industry and levels and trends in consumption, imports and exports.

To determine the investment climate, the corporation will analyse the impact of various factors such as; political stability, nationalism and government policies such as receptivity and special incentives to foreign investors, including tax concessions and low interest loans; whether there are laws restricting the repatriation of earnings, high tariffs and import and exchange restrictions etc.(D. Nabudere ,1977) . High tariffs and import restriction as already pointed out, may attract investors as they help to establish a local plant. The analysis of transport costs, taxes, production cost and cost of production factors such as wages and rent will help the company determine whether it is worthwhile investing.

A close examination of the US direct investment and the direct investment of the European and Japanese monopolies has been testifiable. Investments in Europe, Canada, Japan and US earn about 6-8% where those in the third world, Asia (32%), Africa (29%) and Latin America (14%) average around 25% (Centre for TNCs, 1986-7). The basic aspiration of the MNC are also interalia unregulated economic growth, profit maximization, capital intensive technology and high consumption and they have a very low concert for social justice, ecological balance and economic wellbeing (R.A Falk, 1990).

The MNCs may have some advantages over states in its approach to social forces leading to a new system of world order. For the first time in history, managerial skills and technology make the management of the globe as an integrated unit of genuine possibility. Its purpose include transnational effort to adapt corporate capitalism to changing economic and political forces to ensure capitalism to changing economic and political forces to ensure capitalism's future in non-territorially oriented economy facing

19

possible conflicts with territorially based national government dispossessed classes (R.A Falk, 1990). MNCs place less emphasis on the interest of one state in the system or the well being of its domestic population than national governments. Despite the technologies possessed by the advanced economies the MNCs presence in third world economies only creates technologically dependence.

In Nigeria for instance, despite apparently favourable capital flows, information available indicates that far from having a net positive effect on capital accumulation, MNCs have tended to promote the decapitalization of the host economies. Also, despite the apparent net inflows in the years 1971-79 the picture may be different if the covert transfers such as result from price manipulation, payment for second hand or dilapidated equipments and machines reconditioned and presented as new, and fraudulent transfer such as occurred with the Johnson Mathey Bank (JMB) involving multi-billion naira fraud as well as many other cases revealed by special tribunals set up since the Buhari administration over invoicing sale of naira in western markets at a very low rates are taken into account (NIIA,1989).

It has been maintained that the major interest of these Nigerian shareholders, directors, managers, landlords, transporters, dealers, lawyers, accountant and contractors is to make as much money possible and keep most of them abroad in the countries of these multi-nationals. It is also important to indicate the sectors in which the foreign direct investment has tended to contract in order to establish their pervasive impact on the political economy. Cumulative investment in the manufacturing and processing sector increased from N506.2 million in 1975 to N 550.7 million in 1976 and N703.8 million in 19977 (NIIA.1989).

Overwhelmingly, evidence exist to show that the claim that they are agents of industrialization and technological development can be amply faulted, following the policy of import substitution instituted during the colonial period, when there was absence of viable industrial and technological base, the post independence era had witnessed no major breakthrough in technology being dominated by low technology and light industries. The dependence, which is more acute in high intensive technology sector like oil and iron and steel, is replicated by and large in other industrial sectors including the construction of automobiles sectors where imported inputs constitute from 60-80% of inputs. Under the circumstances it not surprising that the auto industries in which local participation has gone up to 60% are able to hold the Nigerian government to ransom by frequent excessive increase in prices, shutdown and retrenchment.

Despite the involvement of the MNCs in these sectors, Nigeria remains technologically under-developed. The blame however cannot be placed solely on the MNCs but be shared with the role played by the Nigerian state and the ruling class, which by various accommodative policies have encouraged this pattern of development since independence. They have done so by promoting the illusion that MNCs are interested in developing the technological capacity of Nigerians and by offering them incentives, fiscal and otherwise and other forms of protection, which encouraged inefficient quota system which is apparently intended to stimulate local training and progressive replacement of expatriates by Nigerians and by a series of policies and legislation which emphasize transfer rather than local development of technology (NIIA, 1989).

More important, the list of directors and shareholders in joint ventures in which the MNCs control is a list of retired permanent secretaries, retired military generals, traditional rulers, top government functionaries all of whom strategically located in the power structure or have substantial influence in government policies or access to decision makers. Allies of foreign capitalist, these petty bourgeoisies serve the interest of the MNCs as against national interest since despite independence the centre for deliberation still lies outside. They, as clients of the state and the MNCs, from the third arm of the new colonial triangle and are not in a position to quantitatively shape the political economy (NIIA, 1989).

The MNCs expansion could not have occurred on the scale achieved without the financial contribution of the world's international banks. Indeed, the Trans-National Bank (TNB) has itself also become a major actor in the global economy. IN 1985, the combined assets of the world's twenty five largest banks grow to $2.6 trillion a figure nearly triple the combined sales of twenty five largest industrial firms. Reflecting trends elsewhere in the transforming global economy, in 1985 five of the ten largest banks were Japanese, whereas in 1978 only one of the ten largest was Japanese (centre on transnational corporations, 1987: 40).

Regulating activities of MNCs in the third world countries quite differs from that of the industrialised states. Host governments in industrialised states are frequently more concerned about the integration of foreign owned branch into domestic economy than they are about their location. MNCs, which make substantial domestic sales involving a significant import, content, notably in high technology sectors; can create adverse balance of payment effects. In so far as branch plant rely on flows of in-house goods and services provided by the corporate parent, they create fewer demands for output of local firms (Britton,1976) and generate employment characterized by a truncated occupational profile, one which lacks serious managerial positions on research and development (R & D) functions (Hayter,1982).

Nations such as the United Kingdom and France are in a stronger position to exert pressure on MNCs to organize their business in ways, which promote national interest of the third world countries. The allocation of public sector spending is itself a powerful instrument to encourage desired patterns of behaviour. The organization of IBM in western Europe represents one response to demands that it act as a ' good corporate citizen' that value added in given country is in fair proportion to IBM sales and bought in parts come from states where there is no direct manufacturing (the economist, 29 October 1977, P.92).

In contrast to the above scenario, most third world states are controlled by MNCs in several aspects. When the trans-national oil companies began to develop the reserves of the middle East in the 1920s, they encountered weak state authorities that granted them concessions, giving them exclusive rights over development of the resource base and making them " The sole arbiter(s) of the volume and nature of investments in host country, the choice of areas for exploitation, the determination of exploration plans, the development of oil fields, the production levels, the size of the necessary production facilities, exportation and transportation capacities, etc. In practical terms this deprived the state the right to interfere in any of these vital matters and limited its role merely to that of collecting taxes" (Alchalabi, 1980).

This is the same with African states especially Nigeria where multi-national oil companies established in the country such as Shell, Chevron, Exxon Mobil and so on explore and exploit oil with their technology.

Multi-nationals companies are coming in from the cold. Government in both rich and poor countries, anxious for new investment to promote jobs and exports, are giving multi-nationals a warmer welcome. The adversarial relationship between states (especially in the third world) and MNCs which characterized much of the 1970s, has softened partly for reasons just cited and partly because governments have become more adept in their dealings with foreign investors. For instance, whereas MNCs are still in position to play one state off against another in seeking investment incentives, the proliferation of corporations capable of operating at a global scale from variety of home countries makes it easier for a potential host country to bargain with the competing would be entrants to its domestic market (Dunning and Stopford, 1983; The economist, 19 February, 1983, P.86). This is just as the case was in Nigeria, when Peugeot Automobile Nigeria (PAN) and several other multi-national automobile companies wanted to invest in the Nigerian market. At that time, only PAN and Volkswagen were granted accreditation to invest. On the other occasion, MNCs have used bribery to influence key foreign officials. The extent of such activities by American firms was unearthed in the aftermath of the Watergate scandal in the United States in the early 1970s. The Securities and Exchange Commission and later a congressional inquiry disclosed improper foreign payments totalling more than $100 million made by one hundred Americans (Cutler, 1978). Multi-nationals are known to enslave third world countries since they exist. The parent companies monopolize key decision like choice of technology, research and development and so on. This process of expanding a company from one country to many countries is the internationalization of capital. But internationalization does not mean that TNCs have no nationality; their nationality is their home country, whose interest they serve most of the time. (Onimode 1975). Choice of technology comes from AP in France with this they monopolize and control key decisions in the subsidiary PAN.

Although, much of the critical literature consider the remission of excessive profits, the key mechanism by which the host country's balance of payment is adversely affected by MNCs. The annual income remissions, R. Vernon argues are insignificant compared to local value added annually by such corporations (cited in Bierkstecker, 1978). Vernon also challenges the capital outflow and technology dependence argument, alleging that the former is fallacious because of its failure to measure the implication of changes to domestic output, whereas the later is subject to an overwhelming propensity on the part of the well-trained and well-informed critics to over simplify the issue and to disregard the non-conforming evidence (Vernon, 1975).

The MNCs power is often alleged to be exercised at great cost to their home or parent countries. MNCs are charged with shifting productive facilities abroad to avoid demands by powerful labour union for higher wages. According to this view, because capital is more mobile than labour, the practice of exporting production from industrially advanced countries to industrially backward countries, where labour is cheap and unions are weak or non-existent is the cause of structural unemployment in the advanced countries. Others contend the nation's balance of payment deficit; create new employment opportunities and promote competition in both domestic and foreign markets (D. Nabudere, 1977). But this is the case of an advanced capitalist state where national interest is also a priority apart from profit maximization.

The economic consequence of MNCs is not always agreed upon. This is perhaps why evaluation does not point to consensus. "It is impossible to reach any general or definite conclusion about overall effect of multinationals on development. The influence of foreign investment varies from country to country, firm to firm and from project to project. Some case studies demonstrate the beneficial impact; others point out the detrimental effects of direct foreign investment" (Sparo, 1985).

The essence of this literature review is to explore the various write-ups and publications that view multi-national corporations as either agents of development or under development.

This research work will concentrate on PAN and its contribution to the Nigerian Development.

CHAPTER THREE

3.0 HISTORICAL BACKGROUND OF PEUGEOT AUTOMOBILE NIGERIA

Peugeot Automobile Nigeria (PAN) is in the business of providing quality vehicles and spare parts to the market through local assemblage and importation of CBUs (completely built units). The Company's assembly plant is situated on a total surface area of 330,000 square meters with a free area of 177,200 square meters. The plant has the capacity to assemble 264 cars per day and provide a wide range of cars to the market.

Being Nigeria's largest car plant, PAN stands to benefit greatly from Nigeria's fast growing consumer market and access to regional markets. In order to ensure full coverage of this potential market, the company is focusing on serving and dominating the Nigerian and West African markets in the short to medium term.

In 1957 hundred units of Peugeot cars were imported by individuals into Nigeria. Two years later, SCOA was appointed soles agent for Peugeot cars and she imported the first set of 403 cars.

Since independence in 1960 however, the growth rate of the Nigerian economy had increased to the proportion that the number of imported cars can no longer cope with the demand. In essence the demand for Peugeot cars in Nigeria was higher than its supply. Recognizing the need therefore to meet up with that demand, the then military government of Nigeria under the leadership of Yakubu Gowon negotiated with Automobile Peugeot of France, which is the parent company of Peugeot Automobile Nigeria (PAN) for the setting up of an assembly plant in Nigeria. There were also agreements reached between both parties, which among others were research and development that allows technological innovations and introduction of transfer of advanced technology to the host country. That is the transfer of technology which will make possible the production of Automobiles in Nigeria by Nigerians gradually. On December 1972, Peugeot Automobile Nigeria (PAN) was incorporated with an authorised share capital of three million naira (N3, 000,000.00) and paid up capital of two million naira (N2, 000,000.00). That was to increase with the growth and transformation of the company and the economy.

On March 14, 1975, the assembly plant in Kaduna was commissioned by the then Head of State General Yakubu Gowon, and first Nigerian assembled car rolled out of the plant. Since then PAN's annual turnover has seen remarkable growth from N88.4 million in 1975 to N493.6 million in 1984 with a declared profit of N28 million in that year. This is a clear indication that production at the plant has tremendously increased year after year. For example, whereas the year 1975 saw a production of 2,592 cars, it had risen more than ten-fold to 59,490 in 1981. It however fell sharply in 1984/85 due to the co-existence of the unhealthy state of the nation's economy and less demand resulting to too costly Peugeot cars. But since its inception, PAN has turned out over 370,000 cars within a decade.

The Peugeot has gone through to forms of investment in Nigeria. At first the wealthy individuals dealing with the importation of Peugeot cars and SCOA taking their place to do the same were all engaged in portfolio investment. This was to change as Automobile Peugeot (AP) established its subsidiary in Nigeria, which took the form of foreign direct investment.

The company's equity structure stands at:

- Federal Government of Nigeria   35%
- Kaduna State Government   4.7%
- Katsina State Government   5.3%

27

- Nigerian Industrial Development Bank   5%
- Nigerian Distributors   10%
- Automobile Peugeot France   40%

(Source: Office of Public Relation Manager PAN)

In December 2006, ASD Motors Limited, Peugeot's largest dealership in Nigeria, completed its acquisition of a 54.87 % stake in PAN under the Federal Government's privatization policy. ASD acquired 30% of Automobile Peugeot France's 40% stake and 24.87% of the Nigerian government's 34.87 % share, becoming the firm's new core investor. Below is the latest ownership structure.

Ownership Structure

ASD Group	54.87%
Federal Ministry of Finance Inc.	10%
Automobile Peugeot France	10%
Katsina State	5.3%
SCOA Nigeria Plc	5%
UTC Nigeria Plc	5%
Bank of Industry	5%
Kaduna State	4.83%

(Source: PAN Public Relations Office)

The Nigerian Distributors of Peugeot are located in various part of the country, they are:

- Abadat Motors, Abuja
- AC OKOCHA Motors, Abuja
- A.J Adisco, Ilorin, Kwara

- ASAO Motors, Lagos

- ASD Motors Kaduna and Abuja

- Auto Star Gallery, Enugu

- Capital City Auto, Enugu

- CFAO Motors, Ijora Lagos and Port Harcourt

- Germaine Auto Centre, Victoria Island, Lagos

- Kaura Motors, Kaduna

- Madunka Motors, Kaduna

- Mingi Motors, Port Harcourt

- N.M.I Motors, Lagos, Kano, Abuja

- Oluwalogbon Motors, Victoria Island Lagos

- Paki Motors, Kano

- SCOA Motors, Lagos, Kano, Kaduna, Port Harcourt

- Unbright Motors, Benin City, Edo

The capital inflow of the company varies each year. As earlier stated, Multi-nationals avoid talking about tax evasion, capital inflow and so on.

3.1 OBJECTIVES OF PEUGEOT AUTOMOBILE NIGERIA

The company has set of objectives. Some are in connection with the agreement made between it and the government of Nigeria when it was to be established while others are in line with capital intensive business. The objectives in line with France-Nigeria agreement have not been achieved.

The objectives are:

- Technology transfers from Automobile Peugeot (AP) France to Peugeot Automobile Nigeria (PAN), so that local production of Peugeot vehicles in the country is achieved.
- Enhancement of capacity utilization
- Increase in productive output
- Introduction and transfer of technology and mainly to expand the market for its products in the country.

The control of PAN comes from its parent company AP. Although PAN has board of directors, which include a Chairman, Directors and Managing Director, The present Chairman like previous ones is a member of the ruling class and local elite, who is able to some extent influence government policies regarding the company.

3.2 ORGANIZATIONAL STRUCTURE

The company's policy issues are handled by a board of Directors headed by a chairman who is always from the elite or ruling class, while the General management structure is headed by a Managing Director, assisted by a Deputy. There are five major divisions in the company. They are:

- PERSONNEL

  This is the administrative section of the company. Its primary role is recruitment and maintenance of staff. It consists among other department, public relations and training and development divisions.

- INDUSTRIAL

  This division consists of the factory, which is the assembly plant. It is completely subjected to the policies and programs of Automobile Peugeot (AP), France. This is where production takes place. AP's research and development (R&D) is the backbone of this division.

- LOCAL CONTENT

This division has to do with local raw materials or the objects of locally sourced for production in the company. The division is yet to be improved.

- COMMERCIAL

This is also known as the sales department. It is linked with the marketing section where advertisement is made. It makes consumption possible through the distributors of Peugeot.

- FINANCE

This division is responsible for auditing of financial records for the company.

- PRODUCTION

The production of Peugeot cars in Nigeria is connected with the activities of Automobile Peugeot (AP), which produces the completely knocked down parts (CKD). This CKD is exported to Nigeria for completion of production by assembling it to finished car. PAN requires CKD parts, human labour, technology and locally sourced component parts to complete production.

The completely knocked down parts (CKD) include among other things the following:

- Alternator
- Cylinder head
- Master cylinder
- Brakes
- Release bearings

- Steering

- Shaft

- Carburettor

- Clutch

- Pump

- Speedometer

- Hardware

- Hose clamps

- Transmission cases

- Suspension bushes

- Radio

- Ignition

- Flywheel

- Radiator

- Under body coating gasket

The CKD parts constitute more than 75% of the components, which are produced in AP, France, and the other components constituting 24% which are produced and supplied locally are as follows:

- Michelin tyres in Port-Harcourt

- Exhaust pipes, seat frames from SHEPERT, Kaduna

- Wheel covers, mirrors from CHIEME IMD Aba.

- Cast Aluminium parts from AUTO COMPONENT LIMITED

- NASCO carpets from Jos

- Metal panel, spare wheel covers from CHUCKS METAL CONSTRUCTION, Kaduna

- Foot mats for 504, 306 and 406 from Nasco Carpets jos

  (Source: Office of head of industrial training PAN)

Over the years, production in PAN had risen and had declined, with demand for the product pointed to high cost of Peugeot cars. Technology, seen as the tool for efficient process of production did not help matters. In 2001 PAN introduced the "Numerically controlled blanking machine" otherwise known as LVD. The machine is a product obtained from research and development of AP, France. PAN spent more than 600 million naira for its acquisition. The machine is installed for the purpose of producing parts locally in order to reduce importation of CKD parts. It is capable of cutting on flat sheet up to a maximum of 6mm thickness within an area of 1m2.

PAN, between the years 1998 to 1999 invested more than 700 million naira as claimed to improve the quality of its products and enhance capacity utilization (PAN News, 2001).

CHAPTER FOUR

4.0 THE IMPACT OF PEUGEOT AUTOMOBILE NIGERIA (PAN) ON NIGERIA'S DEVELOPMENT.

The world capitalist system gave rise to the Nigerian economic dependence through the former's domination and exploitation of the later. The Nigerian economy is dependent on finished products from its raw materials exploited by the capitalist states. Huge foreign investments are responsible for the Nigerian economic dependence. Multi-national corporations (MNCs) are known to take part actively in such foreign investments and PAN is one of such MNCs operating in Nigeria.

The large market for its products in the Nigerian economy and the cheap labour attracted the company to invest. Nigerian government is the largest consumer; purchasing more than 70% of what is produced annually.

With the system of production which completely knocked down (CKD) parts are imported from France before assembling in Nigeria, there is unfavourable balance of payment affecting the Nigerian economy because the foreign exchange plays a vital role in such activity. In essence the Nigerian economy devotes resources to the purchase of CKD parts which favours the French economy at the expense of the host country.

Apart from the inequalities and balance of payment problems in the Nigerian economy created by PAN, there are other impacts such as technological dependence on foreign inputs and hence causing problems in industrialization of Nigeria, Import Substitution Industrialization Strategy has gone nowhere as the steel industries are not made to function and the economy is a victim of decapitalization. Also PAN has created international division of labour between France and Nigeria.

4.1 PEUGEOT AUTOMOBILE NIGERIA (PAN) AND IMPORT SUBSTITUTION

Peugeot has maintained monopoly in the automobile sector for quite some time now. This is mainly because the Nigerian Government patronizes their vehicles. Most of the Peugeot vehicles produced by PAN are bought by Nigerian Government.

The other automobile company Volkswagen, that existed the same time with PAN has collapsed, may be if it had been enjoying government patronage it would have been existing. Peugeot products are beyond the reach of an average Nigerians. It is only the wealthy and the government that can afford such vehicles.

In the period of independence when the policy of import substitution was launched, the Nigerian economy was dominated by a relatively small number of merchant companies. In the 1980s the automobile industry was dominated by two multi-nationals, Volkswagen and PAN. PAN has financial investment in AP France from where it imports CKD parts and does not wish to encourage the development of indigenous industries. In addition the import of CKD to Nigeria makes AP's export more profitable.

More so, PAN wields a strong partnership with another French company Michelin. Michelin supplies PAN with Tyres. This partnership has also contributed to the failure of import substitution industrialization and enhanced monopoly in Nigeria.

The Iron and Steel industry, the Warri steel plant and the uncompleted Ajaokuta steel industry all would have been backup industries for car manufacture that will halt the importation of CKD parts from France. The Warri Steel plant for instance comprises all production units such as smelting, steel plant and rolling mill. The iron ore will be imported from other African states and Brazil. Later it is planned that domestic ore will be needed which is available in Jos.

Furthermore, the newly introduced numerically controlled blanking machine otherwise known as LVD is installed for the purpose of producing body parts in order to reduce the importation of CKD; it is capable of cutting out any shape on flat sheet up to a maximum of 6mm thickness within an area of 1m2. This means that millions of dollars spent on building the Warri and Ajaokuta Steel plants have not yielded any positive result. The LVD is a French technology and its introduction in Nigeria means that local production of automobiles in the country is not realistic.

4.2 PEUGEOT AUTOMOBILE NIGERIA (PAN) AND EMPLOYMENT GENERATION IN NIGERIA.

Since its inception, PAN has been utilizing human labour for its production. The workforce was once dominated by French nationals (expatriates), later on gradually replaced by indigenous workers. Most of the local staff in company engaged in low skilled labour. Over the years the size of the workforce in the company grew from 691 to 4000 and reduced to 1061 in 1991due to circumstances in the country then.

The personnel and administrative division is area where indigenous workers dominate the most. Like other divisions in the company, the highest ranking official in the administrative division in the company is General Manager who is a Nigerian. Nigerians in the company are engaged in work like typing, weaving, panel beating, welding and general assembling of CKD parts. On the other hand the expatriates engaged in skilled labour in key and sensitive positions. They include Engineers, foremen and co-ordinators. In the year 1998 almost N184 million was set aside by the company for wages, with senior staff and expatriates earning more than 70% of the amount. The trend has changed with the recent privatization of the company. In 2005, after privatisation, the Peugeot Automobile Nigeria (PAN) had 2015 staff but the workforce, five years later, dwindled to 426 workers as at November 29, 2010. The number, two days later, depleted further as 226 workers, in one fell swoop, were given the boot. Below is the table of how the growth of the size of work force has fared over the years:

TABLE I

YEAR	NUMBER OF EMPLOYEES
1993	1578
1994	1488
1995	1550
1996	1093
1997	905
1998	1103
1999	1061
2002	1200
2005	2015
2010	1363

Source: PAN Training Development Division

4.3 PEUGEOT AUTOMOBILE NIGERIA (PAN) AND NIGERIAN TECHNOLOGICAL DEVELOPMENT.

Efficient production in any economy requires technological advancement. Technology plays a vital role in PAN. With technology, productive machinery is involved in producing component parts and making design of vehicles practicable.

Technology stems from research and development (R & D), which is centred at the present company Automobile Peugeot (AP) France. The AP machinery used in a car manufacture and maintenance include:

- The Automatic Transfer Machine (ATM), the developments and improvements of the ATM aim at complete automation for obtaining of improved production in rates and quality without manual aid. The ATM is involved in CKD production and assembling of vehicles in the parent company AP. It is the maker of those inputs required by PAN.

- The Numerically Controlled Blanking Machine (LVD) : This machine is capable of cutting out any shape on flat sheet up to a maximum of 6mm thickness within an area of 1m2. This is the recent imported technology from AP to PAN. It is introduced to reduce the percentage of imported CKD parts.

Others include the DIAG 2000, exhaust gas analysers and a body dozer; also the DIAG2000 multiplex error detector, complete body work alignment and balancing facilities. PAN engages in the training of its local workers on how to use the above machines. Distributors of Peugeot and other maintenance units are equipped with such.

Technology being the instrument of labour is the vital link between labour and objects of labour. In a modern economy in the case of PAN it is technology that makes it possible for the company to apply power to objects of labour and thus to harness nature to meet needs.

Labour and capital are required for production; with the former being the only productive force, while the latter is a pattern of production relations. There exist a relation between the owners of the means of production and the owners of the means of production and the owners of labour who unite through the wage contract. The labourer is the producer while capital in the form of machinery being the means to increase the efficiency of the workers will also pass as a producer.

The labour processes consist of three elements. The first is the labour power, the second is the object of labour and the third is the means of labours.

With the presence of PAN in Nigeria, there exist the international division of labour between France and Nigeria. This is created when AP France manufactures CKD parts and exports them to PAN for complete assembling. In essence an international labour is created between the high technology of the core and the low technology of the periphery. In this respective scenario both form of technologies are products of the French economy through AP, this means that the assembling plant in Nigeria is futile through AP; which is the producer of CKD parts but production machinery such as LVD (Numerically Controlled Blanking Machine) and Automatic transfer machines (ATM). The developments and improvements of the ATM aim at complete improved production in rates and quality without manual aid. The production process of CKD parts skilled labour of AP with the ATM being a product of high technology while the low technology in Nigeria are involved in assembling the CKD parts to complete production.

The labour power comprises of physical, psychological and intellectual capabilities of the worker. This is shared between Nigeria and France. The skilled labour is usually provided by Automobile Peugeot (AP) France and the unskilled labour by Peugeot Automobile Nigeria (PAN) until after the privatization where Nigerians are now in some key positions. The intellectual ability and the technical know-how come from AP France the parent company which includes Peugeot products of many shapes and sizes, engine capacity automation, the machinery to be used by the subsidiary (PAN) and so on.

Secondly, the objects of labour, which are those ingredients to which labour is applied, such as; objects of nature like coal, oil, iron ore , rubber and so on. In essence natural resources are object of labour. The Warri steel plant, the Ajaokuta steel company, the plastic company all in Nigeria have capability to process such objects of labour that will bring an end to importation of completely knock-down (CKD) parts and hence accelerate the local production of Peugeot cars in Nigeria are subjected to serious neglect due to issues best known to the government of Nigeria. The importation of the CKD is further developing France's economy to the detriment of Nigeria's economy.

Thirdly, the means of labour are instruments with which man labours. Means of labour include all tools and other aids for production, such as vehicles, ships which can transport the worker or objects of labour. The machinery and instruments required by labour to produce Peugeot cars are made by sophisticated technology from AP's Research and Development (R & D). These instruments include inter-alia the LVD, ATM, Exhaust gas analyser, multiflex error detector etc.

The table below shows how AP and PAN relate through the three elements of labour.

Table II

	AP FRANCE	PAN
Labour Power	Skilled labour, research and development to produce ATM and LVD in order to produce CKD	Unskilled labour dependent on technology provided by AP. Assembling of CKD parts, panel beating and spraying
Objects Power	Rubber, Plastic, Iron ore	Untapped and Unused natural resources dependent on foreign inputs
Means of Labour	The ATM, LVD, body dozer, DIAG 2000, Exhaust etc.	Nil

Source: PAN

4.4 CAPITAL FLOW

The General Manager Personnel Division of PAN in an interview on the 10th of April 2001, disclosed that the company spent over N11 billion for the importation of completely knock down (CKD) parts. This was during the year of 1998 and 1999. During the same period also the company invested N1.2 billion, from this amount N700 million was to improve the quality of its products and enhance capacity utilization and N500 million was for the state of art paint shop.

The Manager also disclosed that over N20 billion from the sale of PAN's products was realised. These products (Vehicles) were from produced from the CKD parts imported from France worth N11 billion during the periods of 1998 and 1999.

In Nigeria, there is no enforcing law restricting the repatriation of earnings by multi-national corporations (MNCs). Pan is known to make huge profits and its parent company AP France accumulates capital from the CKD parts it produces.

The Nigerian economy benefits from the taxes the government imposes on PAN, even though it is little. More than N300 million was set aside for wages and allowances for the worker during the same period; 1998/1999 with the expatriates and senior staff who constitute a small fraction of the work force having more than 70%. Equally, the volume of Peugeot product in PAN is being determined by the cost of CKD, cost of shipping, labour required for assembling and local components that complete production. The numbers of vehicles produced from 1998 to 1999 were more than 11,000. These periods (1998 and 1999) were made reference with because of their relevance in Peugeot production and sale in Nigeria. The capital invested can be elaborated in the following table.

Table III

	Capital Asset N(million)	Liquid Assets N(million)
AP FRANCE	200	280
PAN	3000	420
Total	500	700

Source: PAN News and Nigerian Industrial development Bank, 2001

The total capital invested was N1, 200, 000,000 and at that period this was a serious investment.

The latest prices of Peugeot vehicle from PAN is as in the Table below:

Model	Range	Engine Capacity	Transmission	public price
206 hatch back	one line	1.4	manual	2.098M
206 hatch back	one line	1.4	auto	2.467M
207 hatch back	trendy	1.4	manual	2.990M
307 hatch back	D.sign	1.6	manual	2.808M
307 hatch back	XR	1.6	manual	3.150M
307 hatch back	XS	1.6	manual	3.255M
307 hatch back	XS	1.6	auto	3.360M
307 hatch back	oxygo	1.6	auto	3.360M
307 hatch back XSi leather		1.6	auto	3.675M
307 hatch back oxygo leather		1.6	auto	3.675M
307 sedan	XR	1.6	manual	3.350M
307 XS		1.6	manual	3.550M
307 XS pack		2.0	auto	3.700M

406 saloon	Comfort	2.0	manual	3.700M
406 saloon	Dynamic	2.0	manual	4.036M
406 saloon	prestige	2.0	manual	4.485M
407 saloon	comfort	2.0	auto	5.100M
407 saloon	Premium	2.0	manual	5.600M
407 saloon	Premium pack	2.0	auto	6.000M
407 saloon	premium V6	3.0	auto	8.740M
407 coupe	premium	3.0	automatic	9.090M
407 wagon	ST Sports	2.0	manual	6.800M
407 wagon	ST Sports pack	2.0	auto	7.200M
407 wagon	ST Sports V6	3.0	auto	8.900M
607 saloon	Pack leather	2.2	manual	7.770M
607 Saloon	pack V6 leather	3.0	auto	10M

M= million in Nigerian Naira

Source: Marketing section, commercial Division, PAN.

The price of any Peugeot unit assembled in Nigeria is determined by the cost of CKD (completely knocked down) unit imported, the local components, tyres from Michelin and labour required to assemble it. By implication the bulk of the money is remitted to the French economy.

The part of capital mentioned that consisted of the capital assets and liquid assets are all referred to as constant capital because the value of these factors of production remains the same through the production process and are merely transformed. These are the objects of labour and means of labour consisting of iron ore, rubber, plastic, LVD and exhaust gas analyser.

The other part of capital is called variable capital. This is a personal factor of production which consists of human labour. This involves wages given to the worker after meeting production in the company. Although the wages earned by workers in PAN is not precisely known, they are paid monthly.

The Nigerian economy is benefitting from taxes imposed on PAN. In the Nigerian context PAN is regarded as a large company that makes a turn-over of billions of Naira.

Another form of capital is circulating capital, which include semi-finished goods. This means that the CKD parts brought into for assembling to make complete Peugeot which equally generate huge amount of money to France is a circulating capital.

4.5 ECONOMIC IMPLICATION OF PEUGEOT AUTOMOBILE NIGERIA (PAN) ON NIGERIA.

This research work adopted the dependency theory as its analytic tool, which stands opposite to the modernization theory. The multi-national corporations (MNCs) are perceived to be agents of development by the modernization school. They claim that MNCs contribute to the development of third world economies through the under writing of research and development that allows technological innovations, introduce and dispensed technology to less-developed states, reduce the costs of goods by encouraging their production according to the principle of comparative advantage.

However, from findings all the above-mentioned positive contributions were found in-adequate as regards PAN. Nigeria is dependent on foreign inputs in the automobile sector. Both the circulating capital and fixed capital are imported from AP France to make production possible in PAN. The CKD parts imported mostly needed locally processed raw materials in them and backup industries to produce such.

The iron and steel industries, Warri steel plant and Ajaokuta steel are all supposed to serve as back-up industries to PAN and their by promoting industrialization in Nigeria. Importation of foreign inputs impedes local industrialization. PAN is not an indigenous automobile company despite the change in shareholding (since more than 70% inputs are coming from France) and yet it has dominated the automobile industry. It is merely an assembling plant relying on CKD parts, which are imported from its parent company; AP France. With the existence of PAN and the current system of its operation, no indigenous automobile company will emerge.

Equally, the back-up industries that are known to be objects of labour will have less attention on them by the Nigerian Government for their completion. Nigeria is only helping to the growth of France's economy to the detriment of its economy.

Technology involved in production of Peugeot vehicles emanated from AP, France. The subsidiary PAN utilizes a small fraction of technology which is also a product of AP, France. This means that the Nigerian economy is dependent on technology and productive machinery for assembling Peugeot vehicles. Technological advancement requires a successful research and development (R & D). AP is engaged in R & D and after utilization of its products and machinery and improvement is done on them, and Nigerian economy has aided in consuming such machinery.

Furthermore, the Nigerian economy is a third world economy requiring a labour –intensive technology to help develop its economy to some extent. However the technology introduced to the country by PAN is capital intensive.

The most essential issue in foreign investment is capital. The completely knocked down (CKD) part which is a circulating capital and technology, which is fixed capital, cannot be acquired without capital cash. As this research earlier showed, capital worth N1.2 billion was invested during the period 1998 and 1999, a total of N28 billion was involved as capital flow for those two years. CKD worth N11.340 billion was imported and this amount goes to France.

Apart from the N11.340 billion taken to France for CKD, AP also realised N3.6 billion from the profit generated.

In contrast, the Nigerian government is the biggest loser in the venture since it tries to save the company by patronizing Peugeot vehicles. Apart from N11. 340 billion spent on CKD and huge profit generated, the Nigerian government in a bid to save the company from collapse as did to Volkswagen in the some years back, spends extravagantly on Peugeot vehicles for government officials, lawmakers and members of the judiciary. An example is between the year 1999 and 2001 where each of the 109 senators got two Peugeot cars. This amounted to total of N518 million not to talk about ministers who are allocated more than two Peugeot vehicles.

With this development the so called free market economy as advocated by laissez-faire economics has been hampered by government. More so the Peugeot vehicles assembled in PAN are only consumed in Nigeria. The company does not engage in exporting the products and thereby not a source of foreign exchange for the Nigerian economy. Instead capital leaves the Nigerian economy for the French economy, thereby making France to purge ahead and widen the gap between it and Nigeria. Just as the mercantilist have advocated for their economy during the era gold standard. A state should acquire as much gold as possible by practising and operating an export economy. Mercantilist also maintained that an economy should make a favourable balance of payment on international trade at the expense of the other party. Economic development continues to take place in France through its capitalist imperialism at the expense of Nigeria. In essence PAN is France agent of exploitation in Nigeria.

The company has also a comfortable stay in Nigeria due to the fact that the class of the petty bourgeois and compradors serve as agents of multi-national corporations (MNCs) and the western bourgeoisie. There is a reciprocal relationship between these classes and PAN. Firstly, the petty bourgeois influence policies that favour PAN because they constitute the ruling class in the society. For instance, government's policy on the ban on " Tokumbo" cars that have spent some certain number of years, since AP France's production was not to help Nigeria's industrialization process but to force indigenes of the country to patronize PAN vehicles in order for them to maximize profit and repatriate to their country. In turn, the company appoints any member of the ruling class as its president. Secondly the petty bourgeois are of two categories. The first comprise of distributors of Peugeot vehicles and the second comprise of importers of other second hand vehicles. The distributors of Peugeot rely on the company to produce before they can distribute the vehicles while vehicles dealers of the second hand type sees PAN as an adversary that might keep them out of business.

The indigenous suppliers of the locally manufactured components that make that make the vehicles which constitute about 20% of the car see the existence of PAN as not a bad idea after all they derive capital from the business.

However, the local components in value terms constitute not up to 8% , this means that exploitation takes place in this situation. The value of the local component per unit compared to the value of CKD parts imported from France is negligible.

To cap it all, the parent company AP, France invested little and gained much. In the period of 1998 and 1999 combined AP invested N480 million and derived N14 billion while the Nigerian economy invested N720 million for the same purpose and also spent N11 billion for the importation of CKD parts and derived N11, 314 billion from the sale of vehicles and

taxes paid to it. This analysis is enough for the research to view PAN as having a negative

impact on the Nigerian economy.

CHAPTER 5

5.0 SUMMARY, CONCLUSION AND RECOMMENDATION

5.1 SUMMARY

The Nigerian economy is subjected to imperialist control by western world and also integrated into international capitalist economy system, purposely to serve the dominant interest of international capitalist states.

Almost all the sectors of the Nigerian economy are controlled by foreign investors who together with the petty bourgeois elements exploit the working class and drain the economic surpluses emanating from investments. It is in other words, imperialism taking another approach from colonialism to foreign investments. This foreign investment is institutionalized by the large corporations of the advanced capitalist states called the multi-national corporations (MNCs). These MNCs establish subsidiaries in third world economies including Nigeria.

One of the multi-nationals present in Nigeria is Peugeot Automobile Nigeria (PAN) which is subsidiary of Automobile Peugeot (AP), France. This company serves as a mere assembly plant for automobiles in the country. The parent company AP saw Nigeria as a market for its products, so the need to establish a subsidiary arose and negotiations between France and Nigeria took place. The agreements include gradual transfer of technology within a very short time possibly ten years. Another included under writing research and development and also full production of Peugeot vehicles. All these were however not complied with as completely knocked down (CKD) parts are still being imported from France with a very large capital devoted. Inappropriate technology is still been introduced through importation of machinery.

The company, which come to into being in Nigeria in 1975, has made Nigeria economy so dependent that it has hindered the import substitution industrialization strategy from becoming a reality. Industries such as that of iron and steel, Warri steel plant and Ajaokuta are supposed to serve as back up industries and grow with automobile industrialization. Instead, the Nigerian economy is contributing positively to both the French automobile industry and technology and giving less emphasis and deriving less resource to the development of its own industries.

It has been discovered that MNCs make confidential their activities especially if it has to do with capital. They are known to evade evading tax or manipulating prices of their commodities. However, in PAN some data were able to be collected by this research work. Between the period of 1998 and 1999, PAN invested over N1 billion with N480 million coming from foreign capital and N720 million from indigenous capital. It was also discovered that the amount of more than N10 billion was devoted to importation of foreign inputs called completely knocked down (CKD) parts, sales worth N20 billion was made from the assembled CKD. The N20 billion was made from N10 billion worth CKD together with locally supplied components, labour required in assembling and tax. The local components quantitatively constitute more than 20%. However, its cost compared to the foreign inputs and cost of finished vehicle constitutes not more than 5%.

In the final analysis, the research discovered that PAN repatriates huge profit to AP France. During the period 1998 and 1999, PAN has made up to 14 billion from Nigeria, Nigeria economy only benefit from the tax. It gained N314 million from tax and the Nigerian government having gained a little from the business, spends extravagantly to purchase Peugeot vehicles, PAN has gained monopoly in the automobile sector.

However, for the local supplies of local components the existence of PAN has given Jobs and equally generated employment for Nigerians regardless of the size of workforce in it. The petty bourgeoisies and compradors also play a vital role in the activities of PAN by influencing government policies that favour the company.

5.2 CONCLUSION

Nigeria's economic dependence has been deeply entrenched through huge foreign investments, the solicitation and acceptance of foreign technical assistance and loan from external sources and maintenance of cultural, social and educational ties. The implication of Nigeria's economic dependence are so far reaching and devastating. It easily permits the numerous investors to repatriate their huge profit, thereby helping to develop their own countries and in the process, under developing the host countries.

With reference to the natural resources that have been identified and exploited, the country's benefit from the exploitation have not been maximized as a result of the method of exploitation and utilization. Most of the resources are explored and exploited by foreign companies, sold cheaply and exported to foreign countries as raw materials where they are being processed into finished goods and then imported by Nigeria at exorbitant prices.

This research project has come to the conclusion that PAN is an agent of absolute repatriation of capital and stifling the emergence and growth of local firms in the automobile sector.

To some extent PAN has a very little positive impact on the Nigerian economy as far as employment of indigenous workers is concerned. The company had employed local workers since its inception even though the labour in Nigeria is cheap and that is another area of exploitation. From these cheap labours PAN is able to appropriate surplus and huge profit.

In the Automobile Sector, PAN has made Nigeria a technologically dependent state and despite raw materials available in the country and initiatives to build back-up industries to cater for inputs that will feed the automobile sector, the economy is still dependent on foreign outputs. The Nigerian economy is a dependent economy, becoming a market for foreign products. Nigeria should know better the technology that is good for it economy, because the technology introduced by PAN to the country is inappropriate like other MNCs do in third world countries. PAN's technology is capital intensive rather than labour intensive. This in a nutshell is a strategy to make more money for their economy. Furthermore, the tax imposed on PAN is very minimal compared to its turnover and profit yearly. This means that imperialism exists in Nigeria and PAN is an agent for promoting imperialism in the country. It is however not too late to alleviate the status quo, but definitely not to eradicate the level of dependence and exploitation in the economy; this could be done by adopting the Chinese approach. Nigeria closing her boarders to the outside world for sometime in isolation and seeing what it can do without any interference from other states. Perhaps this could be the only way out of what might be termed as "Modernized Slavery".

5.3 RECOMMENDATIONS

In view o f the aforementioned analysis, the following recommendations are made:

- Committed approaches should be taken to transform the automobile industry in Nigeria.
- Resources should be devoted for Research and Development (R & D) especially in automobile design and construction.
- A long term plan should be put in place of the sustenance and advancement of the research findings.

In the case of the present day automobile sector in Nigeria, the country sees importation of technology and relying on foreign architects in R & D from advanced capitalist economies as technological advancement. So long as PAN is in Nigeria, industrial growth in the automobile sector will never take place and Nigeria will continue to rely on CKD and technology and this is not better than importing Second hand vehicles which is within the reach to many Nigerians, than the locally assembled Peugeot cars.

The issue is, whether it is going to take Nigeria 100 years to industrialised, the fact is that this generation does not have to witness the positive result of the industrial policies and programmes. Just like the common thing in Nigeria where policies are expected to have impact on the lives of people within few days. It has to be a gradual process. If the present generation does not see the change it does not mean that the policy has failed. This could only be achieved by serious R & D policies.

- The Ajaokuta steel industry, the warri steel plant and the iron and steel industry should be completed. They are to serve as backing industries to the automobile sector and should provide average percentage of component parts especially flat sheets. Those that cannot be immediately acquired should be imported in the most minimal quantity possible and as R & D goes on, gradual reduction of these imported inputs will be replaced by products of R & D.

- Government should adopt a policy which will drastically bring to an end the importation of used cars and citizens should patronize locally manufactured cars. Imposition of high import duties to discourage this consumption should be introduced.

- The import substitution strategy especially in the automobile industry should be well implemented because it is one the strategies that will enhance industrialization in the country.

- Education sector should be given priority for the optimal utilization of human labour.

- Stimulating the rapid implementation of the local content policy of the country, especially in the extractive and construction industries sub-sector by forming partnership/linkages that engender the learning and transfer of technology process.

- Basic infrastructural development should be done for easy siting of industries and proximity to sources of raw materials for manufacturing industries should be considered.

There is need to integrate technological considerations into the development planning process because a country's industrial competitiveness depends to a large extent on its level and the quality of its managerial resources. In other words, as industrial structures become more complex and international competition more intense, these economies will need more advanced managerial skills, including marketing and finance, to run their industrial enterprise.

BIBLIOGRAPHY

Akec 1981: "A Political Economy of Africa, Longman inc"., Nigeria, pp. 10-11, 108-9, 137-8.

Anthony Goerzen and Shige Makino (2007) - Multinational corporation internationalization in the service sector: a study of Japanese trading companies, Journal of International Business Studies (2007) 38, 1149–1169

Kindle Berger, C.P, 1969. "The Theory of Direct Investment" American Business Abroad. New Heaven yale, University Press, p.35.

Malcolm Tatum, 2010 - www.wisegeek.com/what-is-a-multinational corporation.htm

Nabudere D, 1997: "The public Economy of Imperialism" Daresalam Zed inc. pp 185-192.

Offion D.A, 1980: " Imperialism and Dependency: Fourth Dimension Publishers p,15.

Onimode B, 1989: "Nigerian International Economic Relations NIIA pp. 117-160.

PAN News, 2001: "Public Relations department;PAN

PAN News Magazine, 2002: "NO. 96, ISSN/01893396 January/March 2002.

Peugeot Automobile Nigeria, 2001: "The Manager Personnel and Administration on April 10th 2001, A local Engineeer of the Maintenance Department, Local Content Division PAN April 24th 2001, Head Industrial Training, Training and Development Division, PAN, April 24th,2001.

Snider D., 1979: "Intoduction to International Economics. Irwin inc, pp.140-147.

Streeten P., 1978: "Foreign Investments, Transnational and Developing Countries. Macmillan Press, pp. 16-46.

Thisday Newspaper, 2001: "The Sunday Newspaper, September 9, 2001.

Wallace I., 1990: " The Global Economic System: Union Hyman University Press, Cambridge, pp. 124-151.

Lightning Source UK Ltd.
Milton Keynes UK
UKHW010919110321
380169UK00001B/161